Growing Readers

Purchased with Smart Start Funds

Thoughts and Feelings

Thoughts *and* Feelings

Glad

Written by Elizabeth Budd
Photos by David M. Budd

The Child's World®, Inc.

Published by The Child's World®, Inc.

Design and Production:
The Creative Spark, San Juan Capistrano, CA

Photos: © 1998 David M. Budd Photography

Library of Congress Cataloging-in-Publication Data

Budd, Elizabeth.
    Glad / by Elizabeth Budd.
       p. cm. — (Thoughts and feelings)
    Includes bibliographical references.
    Summary: Simple rhyming text describes happiness, how it feels,
and what can cause it.
    ISBN 1-56766-669-8 (lib. bdg. : alk. paper)
    1. Happiness in children Juvenile literature. [1. Happiness.]
I. Title. II. Series.
BF723.H37B83   1999
152.4'2—dc21
                                                                    99-28177
                                                                    CIP

6

Today's a great day!
I feel really good!
I studied so hard,
as I knew that I should.

My teacher is happy.
My mom's really proud.
I got a good grade.
I'll shout it out loud!

I feel

GLAD!

11

Mom said Chris could come over to play...

and then my grandpa
is coming to stay.

I feel so glad

16

when my soccer team wins...

17

and I also feel glad
when my little sis grins.

My brand new
computer, brought
home by my dad,

20

is one other good thing
that makes me feel glad.

I'm glad to help mom
by doing a chore,
like picking up toys
or sweeping the floor.

I'm glad when I practice
the music I play.

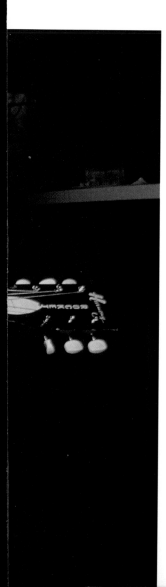

I want to get better,
and this is the way.

I'm glad with my dog,
out for a walk,

26

to chat with my friends,
and to have a good talk.

There's so much that makes me happy, you see.
A good joke can make me giggle with glee.

So if you're ever
feeling angry or sad,
just think of the things
that make you feel

GLAD!

For Further Information and Reading

Books

Kipfer, Barbara Ann. *1,400 Things for Kids to Be Happy About: The Happy Book.* New York: Workman Publishing Co., 1994.

Penner, Fred. *Proud.* Marietta, GA: Longstreet Press, 1997.

Web Sites

For more information about thoughts and feelings:
http://www.kidshealth.org/kid/feeling/

Fairy tales and stories about thoughts and feelings from all over the world: http://www.familyinternet.com/StoryGrowby/